The Sacraments

Text by Inos Biffi
Illustrations by Franco Vignazia

WILLIAM B. EERDMANS PUBLISHING COMPANY
GRAND RAPIDS, MICHIGAN

Contents

Origianlly published as
I Sacramenti, copyright © 1993
Editoriale Jaca Book spa, Milan.

English translation copyright © 1994
by Wm. B. Eerdmans Publishing Co.
255 Jefferson Ave. S.E., Grand Rapids, Mich. 49503

Printed in Italy

Library of Congress Cataloging-in-Publication Data

Biffi, Inos.
[Sacramenti.   English]
The Sacraments / text by Inos Biffi ; illustrations by Franco Vignazia.
          p.   cm.
ISBN 0-8028-3757-3
1. Sacraments—Catholic Church—Juvenile literature.
2. Catholic Church—Doctrines—Juvenile literature.
3. Catholic Church—Liturgy—Juvenile literature.
[1. Sacraments—Catholic Church.   2. Catholic Church—Doctrines.]
I. Vignazia, Franco, ill.   II. Title.
BX2200.B5413   1994
234'.16—dc20   93-39150
                                                                    CIP
                                                                    AC

Imprimatur
in Curia Arch. Mediolani die 28 Septembris 1992
Angelus Mascheroni
provicarius generalis

INOS BIFFI is Professor of Medieval and Systematic Theology at the
Theological University of Northern Italy, Milan.

FRANCO VIGNAZIA lives in Italy and is an illustrator, painter, and
sculptor. He also teaches art in the secondary schools.

Unless otherwise indicated, all Scripture quotations are from the New American Bible,
© 1986 Confraternity of Christian Doctrine, Washington, D.C.

Introduction

This book about the Sacraments is very closely related to the other book in this series about the Apostles' Creed. The Sacraments, as a matter of fact, are rituals that make present in certain ways that which we profess in the Creed. In this book the commentary on the Sacraments is supplemented with clear, simple pictures. Although this combination of explanation and illustration may allow children to grasp some of the concepts on their own, it is essential that they study this book with the guidance of an adult — ideally a parent or a catechist.

It is also essential that children see these Sacraments celebrated in the Church. This will vividly impress these rites on their minds and hearts. With such experiences, augmented by the kind of instruction this book offers, they will be able to begin to understand, appreciate, and desire to participate in these sacred rites, which are the signs, both simple and wonderful, of the Lord's presence in his Church.

The Sacraments:
Acts of Jesus

The Sacraments are visible acts performed by the Church, such as an immersion in water, an anointing with oil, and the celebration of a meal of bread and wine.

But the Sacraments are not only outward actions performed by human beings. They are the actions of Jesus, who instituted them and who makes them have an effect when we perform them. He, together with the Holy Spirit, is truly — even though invisibly — present when the Sacraments are celebrated, just as he is present every time the Church gathers to pray.

On the cross, Jesus gave himself for the salvation of the human race. Through the Sacraments he perpetuates his gift of himself, and our encounter with him is made possible. In the Sacraments, we take part in the passion of Christ, in order to share in his resurrection.

Baptism

It is necessary for us as sinners to be born again "of water and [the] Spirit," Jesus said (John 3:5). For this he has established the sacrament of baptism. The one who administers this sacrament immerses the person being baptized in the baptismal font or pours water on the person's head. During this act, the one performing it says, "I baptize you in the name of the Father, the Son, and the Holy Spirit."

In order to be baptized, it is
necessary to believe in the Gospel.
As a baby, you were baptized in the baptismal font
on the strength of your parents' faith. As you grow
up, their faith will become your own personal faith,
and you will profess it as your own.

When we are baptized, we become children of
God and a new creation, and we begin to be part of

a new family, the Church. The stain of
original sin from Adam is blotted out;
every one of our own personal sins is
pardoned; and it is possible for us to enter
into the kingdom of heaven. Baptism
imprints a permanent sign on our souls
showing that we belong to Jesus Christ;
this is called an indelible character.

Confirmation

Baptism is perfected by the sacrament of confirmation. This sacrament is usually administered by a bishop. He anoints the foreheads of those being confirmed with chrism, which is oil mixed with a fragrance to make a balm. During the anointing, he says, "Be sealed with the gift of the Holy Spirit." He then offers them the same blessing that the risen Lord gave his disciples: "Peace be with you."

Like baptism, confirmation imprints on our souls a permanent sign of belonging to Jesus Christ, since in this sacrament the fullness of the Holy Spirit is poured out on us.

With the grace of the Spirit — which descended upon the apostles on the day of Pentecost, and which we have already received in baptism — we become mature Christians. Our likeness to Christ grows, and we become more intimately a part of his Church.

Confirmation renews and strengthens our commitment to be courageous witnesses of the Gospel in the world, both through our words and through our actions.

The Eucharist

In the celebration of the Eucharist, or Mass, Jesus gives us his body and blood, as food and drink. He established this sacrament at the Last Supper, which he shared with his disciples on the night before he died. When he broke the bread, he said, "Take and eat this is my body, which is given for you. When he blessed the wine, he said,

"Take and drink: this is the chalice of my blood poured out for you and for all so that sins may be forgiven. Do this in memory of me." When we celebrate the Eucharist, we perform an act of obedience and faithfulness to this command of our Lord.

At Mass, through prayer and the working of the Holy Spirit, the bread and the wine are changed, or "transubstantiated," into the body and blood of Jesus. In this way, we are united to the Paschal sacrifice offered by Christ on the cross to his Father for our salvation — so that we too receive the strength to love all others like brothers and sisters.

The celebration of the Eucharist gathers the Faithful together especially on Sunday, the day on which we commemorate the resurrection of the Lord. The priest presides at the sacrament, since he has received the power to do so from Jesus himself. The congregation of the Faithful are not simply spectators; they all participate actively and consciously. The Mass, like all liturgy of the Church, involves the whole people of God: in this rite

all believers are bound together. But not everyone
can receive Holy Communion. Only those who live
in friendship with God — and are not prevented by
serious sin — can approach the table of the Body
of Christ, in anticipation of the heavenly banquet.

Even after the celebration of Mass, Jesus
remains present in the Eucharist. In this way, he
can come in communion to the sick and the dying.
He can also meet his disciples during solemn
Adoration, or be present with them in their
silent personal prayer in the Church.

Reconciliation

SYCOMORVS

Vignazia

When he appeared to the disciples on Easter evening, Jesus gave to them and their successors the Holy Spirit for the forgiveness of sins. He said, "If you forgive the sins of any, they are forgiven" (John 20:23, RSV). During his life Jesus himself had forgiven many sins, such as those of the paralyzed man, and those of Zacchaeus, whom he made come down from the tree.

To obtain forgiveness, we must be truly sorry for our sins, confessing them with honesty to the priest, who absolves them in the name of Christ. And we must also make reparation for our sins, especially through acts of charity and the resolution not to commit them again. The forgiveness of sins is God's greatest cause for rejoicing.

Anointing
of the
Sick

Jesus, who during his life
comforted and healed many who
were sick, has established a special
sacrament for those who are seriously ill
because of disease or aging. The priest
administers this sacrament. He anoints the
body of the sick person with sacred oil
while saying this prayer: "Through this
holy anointing, may the Lord in his
love and mercy help you with the
grace of the Holy Spirit. Amen"

May the Lord who frees you from sin save you and raise you up. Amen."

This sacrament, when received with faith, gives the sick person the comfort of the Lord risen from death. It gives him serenity and trust so that he doesn't allow himself to be pulled down by his suffering. Instead, he is able to unite his suffering from illness with Jesus' passion and offer it for the good of the whole Church. Through this holy anointing, God will grant the sick person the forgiveness of sins and will prepare him for the passage to eternal life; God is also able to restore the grace of health.

Holy Order

The sacrament of Holy Orders is conferred on men through the bishop's laying on of hands and pronouncing of the consecratory prayer. Throu this sacrament some of the Faithful receive the commission to presid over the Christian community, to prea the Gospel, and to celebrate Mass in the name of and w the power of Jesus. The sacrament of Holy Orders, which

(like baptism and confirmation) imprints a permanent mark on the soul, is divided into three degrees. The bishop receives this sacrament in its fullness, and becomes, together with all the other bishops, one of the successors of the apostles. The second degree is received by presbyters, or priests, who are the bishop's closest collaborators. The third degree is received by deacons, who, not being priests and not celebrating Mass, dedicate themselves to serving the Church in various ways: they proclaim and explain the Word of God, they perform certain parts of liturgical rites, and they coordinate many different charitable initiatives.

Those who receive the sacrament of Holy Orders do not replace Jesus Christ but represent him. He acts through them, but always remains the only High Priest.

Matrimony

God himself, who in the beginning created man and woman, has established marriage, through which a couple, united by a mutual, indissoluble, and fruitful love, form a family. The marriage of two disciples of the Lord is a sacrament. The love between two married Christians is a sign of Jesus' love for his Church, and makes that love present. The couple receive from the Lord the grace and the responsibility to love each other

always, to be faithful to each other, to never break the bond of their love, and to give life to children and to educate them.

During the celebration of the marriage, the man and the woman make a mutual commitment to each other: "I take you to be my wife" and "I take you to be my husband." Each of them also makes this vow: "I promise to be true to you in good times and in bad, in sickness and in health. I will love you and honor you all the days of my life."

Jesus prohibits divorce. He says, "That which God has united, man must not divide." Only where there is a mutual, sincere, and abiding love can human life grow and mature.